D1140945

Giftbooks in this series by Helen Exley:

Words on Hope   Words on Joy
Words on Courage   Words on Kindness
Words of Wisdom   Words on Love and Caring

Published simultaneously in 1997 by Exley Publications in
Great Britain, and Exley Giftbooks in the USA.
Copyright © Helen Exley 1997
The moral right of the author has been asserted.

12 11 10 9 8 7 6 5 4 3 2

Edited and pictures selected by Helen Exley
ISBN 1-85015-922-X

Picture research by Image Select International.
Typeset by Delta, Watford.
Printed in China.

**Exley Publications Ltd, 16 Chalk Hill, Watford,
Herts WD1 4BN, UK.
Exley Publications LLC, 232 Madison Avenue,
Suite 1206, NY 10016, USA.**

WORDS ON JOY!

A HELEN EXLEY
GIFTBOOK

EXLEY

NEW YORK • WATFORD, UK

*Write it
on your heart
that every day
is the best day
in the year.*

RALPH
WALDO
EMERSON
(1823-1882)

*W*alk on a rainbow trail;

walk on a trail of song,

and all about you

will be beauty.

There is a way out

of every dark mist,

over a rainbow trail.

NAVAJO SONG

Love the moment,
and the energy
of that moment
will spread beyond
all boundaries.

CORITA KENT.
b.1918

He who bends to himself a Joy
Doth the wingèd
life destroy;
But he who kisses
the Joy as it flies
Lives in Eternity's sunrise.

WILLIAM BLAKE
(1757-1827)

THE MERE SENSE
OF LIVING
IS JOY ENOUGH.

EMILY DICKINSON
(1830-1886)

I do not want change.
I want the same old
and loved things, the same
trees and soft ashgreen;
the turtle-doves,
the blackbirds, the coloured
yellow-hammer sing, sing,
singing so long as there
is light to cast a shadow
on the dial, for such is
the measure of his song,
and I want them
in the same place.

RICHARD JEFFERIES
(1848-1887)

I would look up –
and laugh – and love –
and lift.

HOWARD ARNOLD WALTER

O wonderful, wonderful,
and most wonderful
wonderful, and yet again
wonderful, and after
that out of all whooping!

WILLIAM SHAKESPEARE
(1564-1616)

Oh, the wild joys of living!
the leaping from rock to rock...
How good is man's life, the
mere living! how fit to employ
All the heart
and the soul and the senses
forever in joy!

ROBERT BROWNING
(1812-1889)

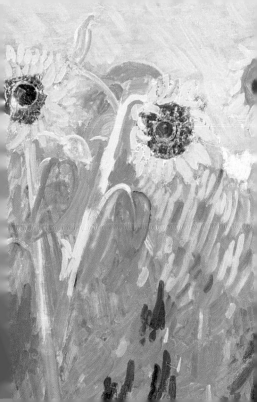

*T*he most evident token
and apparent sign
of true wisdom
is a constant
and unconstrained
rejoicing.

MICHEL DE MONTAIGNE
(1533-1592)

*S*pend all you have

for loveliness,

Buy it and never count

the cost...

And for a breath

of ecstasy

Give all that you have been,

or could be.

SARA TEASDALE

... the little hills rejoice
on every side. The pastures
are clothed with flocks;
the valleys also are covered
over with corn; they shout
for joy, they also sing.

PSALMS 65:12-13

Breathless,
we flung us on the windy hill,
Laughed in the sun,
and kissed the lovely grass.

RUPERT BROOKE
(1887-1915)

A joyful heart is the inevitable result of a heart burning with love.

MOTHER TERESA, b.1910

To be joyful in the universe
is a brave and reckless act.
The courage for joy springs
not from the certainty
of human experience, but the
surprise. Our astonishment at
being loved, our bold willingness
to love in return – these wonders
promise the possibility of
joyfulness,
no matter how often and
how harshly love seems
to be lost.

MOLLY FUMIA

Earth's crammed
with heaven.

ELIZABETH BARRETT BROWNING
(1806-1861)

What I saw was
equal ecstasy:
One universal smile
it seemed of all things.

DANTE
(1265-1321)

My soul's reverence for
creation increases every time
I behold the miracle of a
sunset or the beauty of
the moon.

MAHATMA GANDHI
(1869-1948)

Happiness is essentially
a state of going somewhere,
wholeheartedly,
one directionally,
without regret or
reservation.

WILLIAM SHELDON

Happiness is inward
and not outward; and so
it does not depend
on what we have, but on
what we are.

HENRY VAN DYKE
(1852-1933)

*M*y joy is like spring,
so warm, it makes flowers
bloom in my hands.

THICH NHAT HANH

My heart leaps up
when I behold
A rainbow in the sky:
So was it when my
life began;
So is it now I am a man:
So be it when I shall
grow old,
Or let me die!

WILLIAM WORDSWORTH
(1770-1850)

Happiness is when
everyday things shine
like gold.

PAM BROWN.
b. 1928

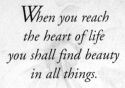

*W*hen you reach
the heart of life
you shall find beauty
in all things.

KAHLIL GIBRAN
(1883-1931)

They seemed to come
suddenly upon happiness
as if they had surprised
a butterfly in the winter
woods....

EDITH WHARTON
(c.1861-1937)

The moments of happiness
we enjoy take us by surprise.
It is not that we seize them,
but that they seize us.

ASHLEY MONTAGU,
b.1905

I slept and dreamed
that life was joy,
I awoke and saw that life
was duty,
I acted, and behold duty
was joy.

RABINDRANATH TAGORE

(1 8 6 1 - 1 9 4 1)

No joy can equal
the joy of serving
others.

SAI BABA

Isn't it a wonderful
morning?
The world looks
like something
God had just imagined
for His own pleasure!

L.M. MONTGOMERY
(1874-1942)

Every day is a birthday;
every moment of it is
new to us; we are born again,
renewed for fresh work
and endeavour.

ISAAC WATTS

The sun does not shine
for a few trees and flowers,
but for the wide
world's joy.

HENRY WARD BEECHER

The same stream of life
that runs through my veins
night and day runs through
the world and dances
in rhythmic measures.

It is the same life
that shoots in joy, through
the dust of the earth
in numberless blades of grass
and breaks into tumultuous
waves of leaves and flowers.

RABINDRANATH TAGORE
(1861-1941)

Whether
seventy
or sixteen,
there can be in
every being's
heart the love
of wonder...
the unfailing
childlike appetite
for what is next,
and a joy of the
game of life.

ULLMAN

I cannot believe
that the unscrutable universe
turns on an axis of suffering;
surely the strange beauty
of the world must somewhere
rest on pure joy!

LOUISE BOGAN
(1897-1970)

Your joy is your sorrow
unmasked.
And the selfsame well
from which your laughter
rises was oftentimes filled
with your tears.

KAHLIL GIBRAN
(1883-1931)

*M*ental sunshine will cause
the flowers of peace,
happiness, and prosperity
to grow upon the face
of the earth.

ANONYMOUS GRAFFITI

I struggle to live for
the beauty of a pansy
for a little black baby's song
for my lover's laugh
I struggle for the blaze of pink
across the evening sky...
I struggle for life and
the pursuit of its happiness
I struggle to fill my house
with joy.

STEPHANIE BYRD

The great sea

Has sent me adrift,

It moves me as the weed in a

great river.

Earth and the great weather

Move me,

Have carried me away

And move my inward parts

with joy.

UVAVNU

Stars over snow,
And in the west a planet
Swinging below a star –
Look for a lovely thing

and you will find it,
It is not far –
It never will be far.

SARA TEASDALE

Above all, let us never
forget that an act of goodness
is in itself an act of happiness.
It is the flower of a long
inner life of joy and
contentment; it tells of
peaceful hours and days
on the sunniest heights
of our soul.

COUNT
MAURICE MAETERLINCK
(1862-1949)

TRUE JOY
IS SERENE.

SENECA
(c.4 B.C.-A.D. 65)

B<small>E GLAD OF LIFE</small>

<small>BECAUSE IT GIVES YOU</small>

<small>THE CHANCE TO LOVE</small>

<small>AND TO WORK AND TO PLAY</small>

<small>AND TO LOOK UP</small>

<small>AT THE STARS.</small>

HENRY VAN DYKE
(1852-1933)

PEOPLE

FROM A PLANET

WITHOUT FLOWERS

WOULD THINK

WE MUST BE MAD

WITH JOY

THE WHOLE TIME

TO HAVE SUCH THINGS

ABOUT US.

IRIS MURDOCH,
b.1919

The longer I live the more
my mind dwells upon
the beauty and wonder
of the world....
I have climbed its mountains,
roamed its forests, sailed
its waters, crossed its deserts, felt
the sting of its frosts,
he oppression of its heats,
he drench of its rains,
the fury of its winds,
and always have beauty
and joy waited upon
my goings and comings.

JOHN BURROUGHS

*F*or the past eighty years I have started each day in the same manner. It is not a mechanical routine but something essential to my daily life. I go to the piano and I play two preludes and fugues of Bach. I cannot think of doing otherwise. It is a sort of benediction on the house. But that is not its only meaning for me. It is a rediscovery of the world of which I have the joy of being a part. It fills

...ne with awareness of the
...wonder of life, with a feeling
...of the incredible marvel of being
...a human being.

PABLO   CASALS
(1 8 7 6 - 1 9 7 3)

*T*oday a new sun rises
for me; everything lives,
everything is animated,
everything seems to speak
to me of my passion,
everything invites me
to cherish it....

ANNE DE LENCLOS
(1616-1706)

'or new, and new, and ever new,
‾he golden bud within the blue;
‚nd every morning seems to say:
"There's something happy
on the way...."

HENRY VAN DYKE
(1852-1933)

Is it so small a thing
to have enjoyed the sun,
to have lived light
in the spring,
to have loved,
to have thought,
to have done?

MATTHEW ARNOLD
(1822-1888)

To see a World in a Grain
of Sand
And a Heaven in a Wild Flower,
Hold infinity in the palm of
your hand
and Eternity in an hour.

WILLIAM BLAKE
(1757-1827)

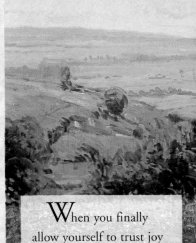

When you finally
allow yourself to trust joy
and embrace it, you will find
you dance with everything.

EMMANUEL

If I were to choose
the sights, the sounds,
the fragrances I most would
want to see and hear and
smell – among all the delights
of the open world – on a final
day on earth, I think I would
choose these: the clear, ethereal
song of a white-throated sparrow
singing at dawn; the smell of
pine trees in the heat of noon;

the lonely calling of
Canada geese; the sight of
a dragon-fly glinting in the
sunshine; the voice of a hermit
thrush far in a darkening wood
at evening; and – most spiritual
and moving of sights – the white
cathedral of a cumulus cloud
floating serenely in the blue
of the sky.

EDWIN WAY TEALE. b.1899

Life is a tragedy

full of joy.

BERNARD
MALAMUD

EGYPTIAN GOD OSIRIS
ASKS THE DECEASED:
"DID YOU BRING JOY?"
"DID YOU FIND JOY?"

Do not linger
to gather flowers
to keep them,
but walk on,
for flowers will
keep themselves
blooming
all your way.

RABINDRANATH TAGORE

(1861-1941)

Acknowledgements: The publishers are grateful for permission to reproduce copyright material. Whilst every effort has been made to trace copyright holders, the publishers would be pleased to hear from any not here acknowledged. SUSAN HILL : Extract from *The Magic Apple Tree* by Susan Hill, published by Minerva, Reed Books. SARA TEASDALE: Extract from *Night* by Sara Teasdale published by Macmillan Publishing Company from *Stars Tonight*. Copyright 1930 by Sara Teasdale Filsinger, renewed 1958 by Guaranty Trust Co. of NY. Extract from *Barter* by Sara Teasdale published by Macmillan Publishing Company from *Collected Poems of Sara Teasdale* Copyright 1917 by Macmillan Publishing Company renewed 1945 by Mamie T. Wheless.

Picture Credits: Exley Publications would like to thank the following organizations and individuals for permission to reproduce their pictures. Whilst every effort has been made to trace copyright holders, the publishers would be pleased to hear from any not here acknowledged. Allied Artists, AISA, Archiv Für Kunst (AKG), Art Resource (AR), Bridgeman Art Library (BAL), Chris Beetles Gallery, Edimedia (EDM), Fine Art Photographic Library (FAP), Superstock (SS).
Cover and title page: © 1997 Barbara Cesery; *Peonies Glace*, SS; page 6: Claude Monet, *Yellow Irises & Pink Cloud*; page 8 and 74/75: © 1997 Bruno Guaitamacchi, *Mountain Flowers*, BAL; page 11: 1997 Ernst Hassebrauk, *Music Lesson*, AKG; page 1

Eugène Henri Cauchois, *Romantic Roses*, FAP; page 14/15: Peder Monsted, *A Winter Landscape*, CCL; page 17: © 1997 Eric Isenburger, *Sunflowers In The Field*, SS; page 18/19: Edgar Degas, *Three dancers in peasant costume*, BAL; page 21: Eugène Louis Gillot, *The Garden in Summer*, EDM; page 23: Helen Allingham, *Summer Flowers*, BAL; page 24: © 1997, Fernando C Amorsolo, *Girl With Fruits*; page 26 and 70/71: Gustav Klimt, *Sunflowers*, AR; page 28: © 1997 Jun Tiongco, *Still Life*; page 30/31: © 1997 Linda Benton, *Poppies*, BAL; page 32/33: © 1997 Karen Armitage, *Chrysanthemum, Snowcap*, BAL; page 34: © 1997 Anna Belle Lee Washington, *Maypoles*, SS; page 37: © 1997 Dorothea Sharp, *Flowerpiece*, BAL; page 39: Claude Monet, *Fields in Spring*, AKG; page 40: Claude Monet, *Iris by the Pond;* page 42/43: © 1997 Timothy Easton, *Iris Field, Storm Gathering*, BAL; page 44: © 1997 Paul Raeschke, *Vase of Lilies*, CCL; page 46/47: Maurice Prendergast, *Summer, New England*, BAL; page 49: © 1997 Lucy Willis, Chris Beetles Gallery; page 51: Warren Smith, Allied Artists; page 52/53: David Cox, *Bettws-Y-Coed*, BAL; page 55: Paul Cézanne, *Vase with Tulips*, AISA; page 56: © 1997 Fritz Freitag, *Happy Winter*, AKG; page 59: © 1997 Barbara Cesery, *Peonies Glace*, SS; page 60: Claude Monet, *Vetheuil 1901*; page 63: © 1997 Richard Carline, *Flowers*, EDM; page 64: Chris Beetles Gallery; page 66/67. © 1997 Robert Sygni, *Pauwi, 1990;* page 68/69: Leon Giran-Max, *In the Poppy Field*, FAP; page 72/73: Vincent Van Gogh, *Olive Trees*.